PANDAS!

PANDAS!

GALLERY BOOKS

An Imprint of W. H. Smith Publishers Inc.

112·Madison Avenue New York NY 10016

THE IMAGE BANK

111 Fifth Avenue New York NY 10003

First published in 1988 in New York by Gallery
Books, an imprint of W.H. Smith Publishers Inc.,
112 Madison Avenue, New York, N.Y. 10016

ISBN 0-8317-6720-0

For rights information about the photographs in
this book please contact:

The Image Bank
111 Fifth Avenue, New York, N.Y. 10003

Manufactured in Singapore

Produced by Robert M. Tod
Art Direction and Design by Mark Weinberg
Assistant Art Direction by Dana Shimizu Lee
Written by Joseph P. Griffith
Edited by Sheila Buff
Photo Research: David Clark
Editorial Assistance: Elizabeth Loonan

The giant panda is not only the

precious property of the Chinese people,

but also a precious natural heritage

of concern to people all over the world.

—*World Wildlife Fund*

The giant panda has long been a symbol of everything cute and cuddly about animals. It is awkward and lumbering and roly-poly, and it seems to look at you with large, soulful eyes. From stuffed animals to Andy Panda cartoons, it is a childhood favorite.

The giant panda has come to symbolize more than that, though. It is a species facing extinction, its natural habitat and food supply threatened. Because it is so endearing and endangered, the conservationist World Wildlife Fund has adopted it as a symbol for all animals that face such danger.

Wherever they go, donated from Chinese zoos or on loan, pandas bring delight to their visitors. Ling-Ling and Hsing-Hsing of the National Zoo in Washington, D.C., the United States' only resident pair, receive annual valentines from schoolchildren and get-well cards when they are ill. Attendance doubled at the Los Angeles Zoo when China loaned a pair to help celebrate the 1984 Olympic Games. When a cub was born in Tokyo's Ueno Zoo in 1986, a contest to name it brought 270,000 suggestions, the winner being Tong (Child). Thirteen thousand

people stood in line to see it, and 200,000 a day called a Dial-a-Panda hotline to hear it squeal.

A highly publicized six-month visit brought two "great bear-cats," as the Chinese call them, from the Beijing Zoo to the New York Zoological Society's Bronx Zoo in April 1987. New York Mayor Edward I. Koch and the society had lobbied the Chinese long and hard for the privilege, and the pair arrived first-class aboard a 747 jetliner. It was estimated that two million people, 2,000 an hour, saw them before they departed for a visit to Busch Gardens in Tampa, Florida.

What is it that makes people go crazy over pandas? Why have they spawned products ranging from hats to swimsuits to postage stamps to cocktails? In 1961 researchers for a British television program found that the animal was among the favorites of children because of its human qualities, it soft roundness and the ease of saying its name, among other things. Dr. Edgar E. Coons, a New York University psychologist, says its cute appearance and clumsy playfulness release "parenting instincts" in humans. Dr. Yi-Fu

Tuan, a University of Wisconsin professor who has written about the relationships between humans and their pets, says pandas' efforts to stand up remind people of a baby's efforts to walk.

Dr. William G. Conway, general director of the Zoological Society and head of the Bronx Zoo, put it another way: "I can't think of any animal that compares. People love penguins, but the interest in pandas is extraordinary. There appears to be an innate response of, 'Oh, isn't this cute?'" Mayor Koch, pleased with the success in obtaining the loan, added, "Pandas are charming. They remind us of our childhood."

The first live panda was brought to the United States in 1936 by Ruth McCombs Harkness, a New York dress designer turned explorer. Her husband, William, was an adventurer who captured wild animals for zoos. They wed in 1934 and he left two weeks later for an extended expedition in the Orient. In Shanghai he and a colorful explorer named Floyd Tangier Smith formulated a plan to capture a giant panda. In the summer of 1935 the expedition was stymied by the Chinese Red Army's Long March, which extended through panda territory. By early 1936, when the Nationalist government granted official permission for them to enter the unstable region, Harkness was dead in Shanghai at age 33 under mysterious circumstances.

Ruth Harkness, who had resented being left behind in the first place, took up her husband's challenge. With little experience other than a love of exotic travel, she arrived in Shanghai and met with Tangier Smith, but they soon quarrelled and parted company. He had shared his information and research, and she agreed to steer clear of the Min Valley, which he planned to explore. She and a Chinese hunter known as Quentin Young set out on a 1,500-mile trip on the Yangtze River, followed by a 300-mile overland trek.

Soon after arriving at the mountain village of Tsaopo near the Min Valley, Young picked up a baby panda in the bamboo thickets. They named it Su Lin ("something very cute"), rushed it to Chengtu and flew to Shanghai, where they tried to circumvent official regulations to remove it from the country. When this was discovered the officials were angered, but Harkness was eventually allowed to sail with Su Lin for San Francisco.

When she arrived on December 18, 1936, the first wave of "pandamonium" began, with reporters and photographers pressing forward to see the infant in its wicker basket. They were setting a precedent that continues to this day whenever pandas are loaned to zoos.

Tangier Smith, meanwhile, had fallen seriously ill, and was convinced that Harkness had invaded his territory. He charged that she had paid one of his hunters to turn over a captured baby panda to her. The press paid little attention to the charge, although evidence has since come to light supporting the possibility. Whether or not Harkness cheated, the fact remains that on a subsequent trip to China, in 1937, she brought back another panda on her own.

Also that year, Harkness turned over Su Lin to Chicago's Brookfield Zoo for $14,000. The animal died in 1938, and scientists were amazed to find in an examination that "she" had been a male. It is difficult to tell the sex of pandas because their sex organs are well-hidden.

More than just having been part of a "first," Ruth Harkness and Su Lin did much to change the emphasis in wildlife studies from big-game hunting to conservation. Even Theodore Roosevelt's sons Kermit and Theodore Jr., who had killed a panda with hunter Quentin Young's brother in 1929, were won over by the cuddly Su Lin.

Panda History and Biology

The giant panda was known in the mysterious East thousands of years before the West found out about it. It was referred to under ancient names in Chinese texts of the twelfth to eighth centuries B.C. One geography book of antiquity referred to it as "a bearlike, black-and-white animal that eats copper and iron," because of its reputation for licking and chewing village cooking pots. The Chinese are thought to have kept the animal in zoos as early as the eleventh century.

European scientists considered the *bei-shung* ("white bear") a myth until 1869, when Père Armand David, a French missionary and naturalist, became the first

Westerner to see one. He understandably classified "the prettiest animal I know" as a bear, christened it *Ursus melanoleucus* (black-and-white bear) and sent skins and bones to the Paris Natural History Museum. But the museum's Professor Alphonse Milne-Edwards studied the bones and teeth and concluded that it was instead a raccoon, reclassifying it *Ailuropoda melanoleuca* (black-and-white panda-foot). Thereby began a scientific debate that has lasted late into the twentieth century.

For years the scientific community generally accepted the giant panda as an "aberrant raccoon." After all, it had evolved, with the lesser or red panda, from a common carnivorous ancestor millions of years before, and the red panda's ancestry was firmly established in the raccoon family. They had been grouped together because of similarities in bone structure, teeth, genitalia and fur color patterns, and Milne-Edwards had postulated that the giant panda's appearance was merely a trace of the ancestor common to bears and raccoons. Some scientists said behavior and biology made the giant panda part of the raccoon family; others

recommended a distinct classification.

In 1964 D. Dwight Davis, curator of mammals at the Field Museum of Natural History in Chicago, published a classic monograph concluding that the panda was a modified, highly specialized bear. His analysis was based on a detailed comparative study of organ systems. He found that the similarities between the giant and lesser pandas resulted more from evolution for similar functions that from common ancestry, and that the two were not closely related genealogically. He said a few minor genetic alternations had produced a panda instead of a bear, and that the biological similarities far outweighed the differences.

Despite Davis's seemingly definitive study, it was more than twenty years before scientists conclusively proved or accepted the theory. In the mid-1980s a team of geneticists headed by Stephen J. O'Brien, co-chairman of the International Committee on Comparative Gene Mapping, conducted a series of tests on giant panda and bear DNA. They used techniques similar to ones they had used to determine the parentage of a cub born to Ling-Ling in

Washington, D.C. Their criteria included comparison of the number and form of chromosomes and the ability of the animals' immune systems to accept or reject foreign tissue.

The fact that bears have 74 chromosomes and giant pandas have only 42 seemed to weigh against a close relationship, but the researchers discovered that the shorter chromosomes of the bear had fused to created fewer, longer panda chromosomes. Meanwhile, only two lesser panda chromosomes were found to have counterparts in either bears or the giant panda, while 14 showed common structure with raccoons. They also found that the bear and raccoon families split on the evolutionary tree more than 40 million years ago, while giant pandas split from bears only about 25 million years ago.

Still, some experts insist that the panda belongs in its own category. George B. Schaller, director for science for Wildlife Conservation International, a division of the New York Zoological Society, said the question is not so easily decided. "All that the biochemical work has shown is that

they are most closely related to the bear," Dr.Schaller said. "Genetically there is only a one-percent difference between a chimpanzee and a human. Can you then say that they are the same?"

The differences Davis had noted between pandas and bears consisted largely of increased size and strength of the teeth and facial muscles brought on by the difficulty of chewing bamboo, the panda's primary food. This in turn changed the shoulders and forelimbs, resulting in the panda's awkward appearance and ambling gait. The animal does not move well and never had to, because for most of its history it lived in a predator-free environment surrounded by its food, which did not try to get away.

When the panda feeds it hold the bamboo in its paws and strips the stalks of its leaves by passing them between its "thumb" and the other five fingers. This thumb is not really a finger at all. Actually, it is a part of the wristbone. In pandas its length almost equals that of the other fingers. The stalks are held in a furrow separating the fingers from the "thumb," which is blessed both with bone for strength and muscles for agility. This setup allows for maximum dexterity in feeding.

Much has been written about the panda's thumb. Davis concluded that genetically it was not of the best design, but that evolution had done what it could with what it was given. The thumb was not designed for the specific task, but the end result worked just the same.

Other differences between pandas and bears are that pandas do not growl; rather, they bark, bleat or make other sounds according to their emotional state. Nor do they hibernate; it is thought that bamboo does not provide enough nutrition or sustenance for that.

The most distinctive thing about the panda is, of course, its coloring. One theory is that the black-and-white markings provide camouflage among the snows and shadows of its natural habitat, but more likely they are a warning to potential predators. Although the animal seems docile, those same jaws that adapted to the crushing of tough bamboo can inflict tremendous bites on enemies. Because of its slowness and difficulty of flight, it is thought that the panda developed the coloration as an advance warning, much like the skunk. In any event its enemies are few—wild dogs, the occasional leopard or bird of prey—and threaten mostly cubs. Its major predator has been man, as we shall see.

The panda looks clumsy, but it is actually fairly agile. It can stand on its stout hind legs, move through the forest or climb trees with ease. It weighs only a few ounces at birth but at maturity, five to six years later, it will weigh 185 to 250 pounds and be five to six feet long. (Weights approaching 400 pounds have been recorded, but these are rare.) Its life span is 20 to 30 years, and it is believed to live longer in the wild than in captivity. It is thought to have generally weak eyesight but acute senses of hearing and smell. Pandas do not like to submerge themself in water and clean themselves mainly scratching, rubbing or licking. They will, however, paddle in a pond, play with water from a hose or sprawl on a block of ice on a hot day.

The panda is active for 14 hours a day, mostly in the morning and evening, resting in the middle of the day and the middle of the night, which can cause disappointment for daytime zoo visitors. It sleeps two to four hours at a stretch. Cubs are more active during the day. Adults will sometimes have periods of activity or inactivity lasting up to six hours. To sleep, they merely find a comfortable spot and lie down; there is no need for a cave or nest. Youngsters love to run, play and climb, but become more sluggish as adults. Springtime is the period of peak activity; females are more sedentary in winter, while males and the young range widely over their territory.

The digestive system of the panda, which is actually a carnivore, is not well suited to the assimilation of bamboo. This accounts for the animal's relatively large droppings and the frequency with which it eliminates them. It does not retain much of the nutrition obtained, and must eat a great deal of bamboo leaves, 22 to 40 pounds a day, to be properly nourished.

The animals are not thought to be highly intelligent, although they can differ as much in personality as humans do. By nature they are solitary, even when together. During the mating season a male will often monitor the movements of other pandas in his vicinity by approaching them but not necessarily establishing direct contact. A type of pecking order establishes some as more dominant than others. Younger pandas sometimes maintain informal relationships.

During confrontations with other pandas or enemies, it may first stare at the aggressor, then rear on its hind legs, growl, swat with its paws and finally lunge. It will wrestle another panda, but in a desperate situation, its ultimate weapons are its dangerous claws and powerful jaws.

Several methods are used to delineate the panda's territory, which normally covers 1.6 to 2.6 square miles. These include biting, clawing or stripping the bark from trees and pawing the ground. By far the most common method is scent-marking, in which a secretion from the tail region is rubbed on trees or other parts of the landscape. A highly glandular patch of naked skin is pressed against the object to be marked, making the place comfortable to the marker and identifiable to others. The short, bushy tail also acts as a brush to spread the scent. The panda may mark the territory in this manner or by urinating or defecating. Sometimes is will use a handstand, lifting its hind legs against a surface before marking it higher above the ground. Scent-marking is used primarily by males to indicate their territory and warn off intruders, but it also indicates the reproductive state. Females, which seldom mark except during fertile periods, can indicate receptivity to male advances in this way. And by sniffing male scents, the female can become more familiar with the male before an encounter.

Mating

Sexual maturity is reached by a panda as early as 3½ years, but normally two to three years later. The genitals are well-hidden, and for this reason zoologists have often been unable to correctly identify the sex of a panda. Females reach their period of greatest receptivity and fertility each year between mid-March and mid-May, with perhaps another, weaker period in autumn. During estrus, or heat, the female loses her appetite, performs more scent-marking and becomes more vocal. Normally loners, pandas seek each other out during this period. Two to five males may compete and

even fight with each other over the affections of a female, with the dominant one winning out, but several may mate with her during a period of estrus. The fighting may be related more to establishing and maintaining dominance than to the particular female.

When scientists know that the peak fertility period of two to seven days is approaching, they monitor protein levels in the urine of captive pandas to determine the precise time of maximum ovulation. Artificial insemination is often used in an attempt to increase the population, because the animals are notoriously lackadaisical about reproducing.

After mating, the male resumes his solitary ways. A pregnant female undergoes what is called delayed implantation, in which the nucleus of the cell that will form the embryo floats in the uterus for 1½ to four months before implanting. It is not known why this takes place, but it is believed to allow the cell to adapt to changes in nutrition and altitude over the panda's range. The characteristic is thought to be a holdover from prehistoric times, when pandas ranged over a much wider area.

The period of gestation is 97 to 163 days. Most cubs are born in August or September. Usually it is a single birth, but there are often twins or even triplets. The process of caring for even a single cub is difficult, so the mother is forced to abandon any others to die, which they almost invariably do. There have been cases of tiny, naked newborns accidentally crushed to death by the mother's weight, which is 900 times greater. The mother fiercely defends her cub in a den she creates from a cave or hollow tree trunk for the purpose of giving birth and raising the baby. She protects the tiny pink newborn in her paw, suckling it, licking it and making sure it is comfortable. After a month, the cub's eyes will finally open. It will weigh two pounds and have a coat of fur, but it will not be able to stand until it is almost three months old. The mother will allow it to move around the den, however.

The mother remains in the den with the cub for four to seven weeks. If she leaves any earlier, even for a short time, the cub faces danger from predators, including martens and weasels. She carries the cub in her mouth until it can stand and walk. A cub that can walk sometimes gets lost and starves, another reason the mother is so protective. It is weaned by eight to nine months old, and strikes out on its own at about 1½ years. By the time it is 2½ it weighs 120 pounds or more, and is able to defend itself.

In captivity, pandas have been the object of great public affection, and their own love stories have been virtual soap operas. The media have reported every intimate detail of their attempts at mating, which have been largely unsuccessful. The objects of much of the attention have been Ling-Ling and Hsing-Hsing, a pair donated by China to the National Zoo in Washington, D.C. in 1972. Especially fascinating and poignant have been Ling-Ling's attempts to breed in the face of advancing age and a rocky relationship with Hsing-Hsing.

By 1985 Ling-Ling had been pregnant twice in the previous two years, but one cub had died of a lung infection hours after birth and the other had been stillborn. Taking no chances, zoo officials kept a supply of frozen semen from Hsing-Hsing and another panda on hand for possible artificial insemination, but when Ling-Ling seemed as though she would not go into heat that year, they gave her hormone treatments. These succeeded in bringing her into heat and she apparently mated, but without issue. Meanwhile, zoos in Mexico City and Tokyo announced that their pandas had produced cubs that survived.

Ling-Ling tried again, and in June 1987 she gave birth to a four-ounce cub in the middle of the night as zoo officials watched on closed-circuit television. The cub was the second of a litter of two; the first had died because of a lack of oxygen. "The world celebrates—and holds its breath," the *New York Times* announced in an editorial.

But the triumph was short-lived; four days later the cub died of an abdominal infection. Ling-Ling seemed resigned to her fate. After the death of her cub in 1984, she had cradled objects as though she were mothering them. This time she merely resumed her normal behavior.

At least there was some cause for hope. In August 1986 the World Wildlife Fund had announced the birth of a 3½-ounce cub at a center it runs in conjunction with China. The organization called the birth a major step toward saving the species. Another panda had been conceived and born using artificial insemination. The center, established in China in 1980, is a kind of "halfway house,"

neither zoo nor wild. The organization said pandas living or born there would more easily adapt to the wild because the artificial habitat closely approximates their wild state.

Conservation

The center is located at the 494,000-acre Wolong Natural Reserve, one of 12 panda preserves in Sichuan, Gansu and Shaanxi provinces, in the Tibetan highlands. All of the remaining 700 or so wild pandas live in these preserves. Dr. Schaller of the New York Zoological Society worked with Hu Jinchu, China's leading panda expert, the Chinese government and the World Wildlife Fund to establish a management strategy to save the animal from extinction and the various other threats it faces. The major ones are lack of success in reproducing, starvation because of periodic die-offs of its bamboo food staple and encroachment upon its habitat from man.

The breeding problem has already been documented. The solution in China has been to closely monitor and attempt to induce breeding, by natural and artificial means, at the so-called "pandaminium." Introducing pandas to the wild after they are raised at the center is the ultimate goal.

Starvation is a more complex problem. The panda eats several species of bamboo that exist at elevations of 6,000 to 12,000 feet. For some reason, these species flower and die every 40 to 50 years, producing seedlings that are too small for the panda to subsist on. The plants take several years to regenerate, and the pandas starve in the meantime. In the mid-1970s, for instance, a mass flowering caused the starvation deaths of 138 pandas.

The efforts of governments, conservation organizations and ordinary citizens in fighting the declines have been at times heroic. The United States Department of the Interior placed the panda on its endangered list in 1985, prohibiting trade in the animal or its by-products. American schoolchildren raised $13,000 in a "Pennies for Pandas" program. The Chinese govenment offered rewards of $100, about a year's salary, to local peasants who rescued pandas or alerted officials when they were in danger. In one dramatic rescue in 1984, a starving panda apparently fell off a cliff, and a peasant and his neighbors loaded it onto a tractor for a 19-hour drive to a government center, where it was saved. Other peasants have slaughtered goats to feed pandas, or led them to bamboo thickets.

Starving animals are placed in holding stations for recovery, then transferred to new habitats with sufficient bamboo. Supplementary food is provided in the form of meat, corn and sugarcane set out near villages and winter wheat planted adjacent to preserves. But these methods are not always easy or successful because of the rugged, remote terrain. One measure being tried is the establishment of corridors between panda habitats. Besides providing for greater ease of feeding, it is hoped tht this will facilitate mating and eliminate future genetic difficulties caused by inbreeding. It would also serve to increase the population of smaller reserves; a population smaller than 20 is given little hope of survival.

The ultimate problem is man. Until the mid-twentieth century he was one of the prime hunters of the panda, for its attractive fur; the Chinese political situation allowed little serious study. Today his adverse effects are felt in more subtle ways. Hunters of other animals sometimes inadvertently kill or capture pandas. Human settlements, logging activities, construction of hydroelectric plants—all conspire to encroach upon their habitat. While acknowledging the panda's plight, the Chinese government has at times assigned priority to the needs of the rapidly growing human population, which needs land and timber. Even the truck traffic from logging operations has frightened pandas to the point that they will not descend from the barren mountains to lower elevations with sufficient food. Many thousands of years ago they ranged from eastern China south to what is now Burma; today they inhabit a fraction of that area. But the government has taken steps to reverse the effects of bad management by banning hunting, grazing, development, farming and burning. Villages have been relocated, bamboo has been replanted, the forest cover is being maintained, poachers have been jailed and protectionist laws are being strictly enforced. Britain's Prince Philip, president of the World Wildlife Fund International, said of the management strategy, "Without this joint effort by the Chinese and the World Wildlife Fund we would be condemning the panda to extinction as surely as if we were to go out and deliberately exterminate them."

The research continues. Chinese and American scientists are conducting a census to discover the true population in the wild, and bamboo is also being surveyed to discover where it must be preserved or replanted. Dr. Schaller has urged that new reserves be created and old ones expanded, that Chinese zoos loan instead of donating pandas and that they improve measures for captive breeding. "This is fairly easy to do if all the dedication the Chinese have devoted to it is implemented," he said.

The agreement between China and the World Wildlife Fund says, "The giant panda is not only the precious property of the Chinese people, but also a precious natural heritage of concern to people all over the world." Dr. Schaller agrees, adding, "By saving the panda, which is a symbol of world conservation, we express our commitment to and faith in the future."

Without this joint effort by the Chinese and the World Wildlife Fund we would be condemning the panda to extinction as surely as if we were to go out and deliberately exterminate them.

—Prince Philip, president, World Wildlife Fund

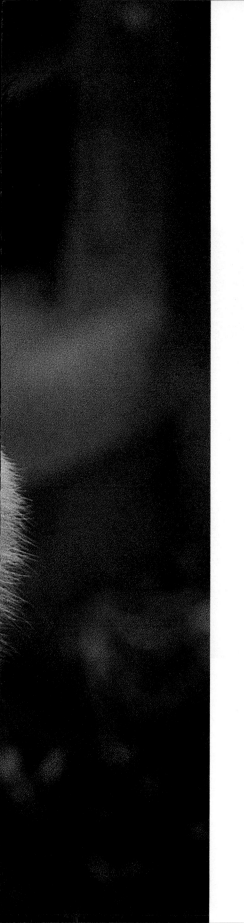

INDEX OF PHOTOGRAPHERS